Integrity Management of Onshore & Offshore Pipelines

J N Agrawal

Made with ♥ on the Notion Press Platform

www.notionpress.com

Table of contents

Preface

This book has been written by me based on my experience in pipeline integrity management for more than 39 years in oil and gas industry in India. I have worked in projects, construction, inspection, operation and maintenance, quality control and audit in oil and gas cross country pipeline. As a consultant in post-retirement period of 6 years, I have carried out pipeline integrity assessments of onshore and offshore pipelines together with prediction of fitness and residual life of pipelines suggesting mitigation measures. In addition, I have also trained integrity engineers.

This book discusses important topics related to pipeline integrity such as integrity management process, threats to pipeline integrity and its assessment, Integrity assessment, tools for integrity assessment and its data analysis, in line inspection, External corrosion and internal corrosion direct assessment, corrosion monitoring, residual life assessment and fitness for purpose, mitigation, intervention and repair etc. Case studies and quiz test have also been included in this book for understanding and testing knowledge of the subject.

I hope that the book will be very useful for asset integrity managers looking after asset integrity and provide inputs for taking decisions in carrying out integrity assessment and taking corrective measures.

For any clarifications and suggestions, please contact me as below:

J N Agrawal
CEO, Corrsol Tech
Author, coach, and trainer
CP Level 4, CP Specialist, ICorr
Mail id: ja02251@gmail.com

About the author

Shri J N Agrawal is B Tech in Electrical Engineering and MBA in Marketing. He has wide experience of more than 39 years in oil and gas cross country pipelines in project management, operation and maintenance and integrity management. His areas of interests are corrosion control, cathodic protection, and integrity management. He is presently engaged in providing consultancy services in above fields. He is also conducting corrosion audit in oil and gas industry and imparting training on cathodic protection and pipeline integrity management. He is CEO of Corrsol Tech. He is ICorr certified CP Level 4, CP specialist. He has contributed many papers in national and international conferences such as CORCON, ASME and others. He has also authored books and guides on CP and Integrity Management of onshore and offshore pipelines. He has founded Association of Corrosion Professionals in 2019 and is now its President.

Chapter 1

Introduction to integrity management

1.1 Integrity: What it is?

"Integrity is defined as ability of an asset to perform its required function effectively and efficiently within its life cycle and beyond protecting people, asset and environment"

Further, simplifying, integrity improves performance of the asset what it is required to perform with optimum efficiency and in the process protects people and environment.

Following components may be attributed to integrity:

1. **Performance** is improved if integrity is maintained
2. **Quality** is to be maintained if integrity is required
3. **Life cycle** is enhanced as integrity is improved
4. **Cost optimization** is the result of improvement of integrity
5. **Safety, health, and environment** are affected as integrity is compromised
6. **Time** is important from the point of view of corrective measures at appropriate time. This effective decision making improves integrity
7. **Brand image** is achieved by integrity improvement

1.2 Codes and regulatory requirements for integrity management:

PNGRB - IMS Regulations 2012

All operators of existing and new natural gas transmission and distribution pipelines shall develop an integrity management program comprising the necessary plans, implementation schedule and assessment of its effectiveness in order to ensure safe and reliable operation of the pipelines.

OISD 226

A comprehensive manual containing program & practices shall be developed for existing pipeline / after construction of the new pipeline to manage pipeline integrity taking intoconsideration consequences, classification / category of pipeline and risk involved in each segment of the pipeline.

ASME B 31.8 S / API 1160

Operator needs to develop and implement an effective integrity management program utilizing proven industry practices and processes.

1.3 Integrity management program elements:

1. Integrity management plan
2. Performance plan
3. Communication plan
4. Management of change plan
5. Quality control plan

1.4 Referred standards

The referred standards for integrity management are as follows:

1. ANSI/ASME B31.8: Gas transmission and distribution piping system
2. ANSI/ASME B 31.4: Pipeline transportation system for liquid hydrocarbon
3. ANSI/ASME B31.8S: Managing system integrity of gas pipeline
4. NACE SP 0207: Performing close interval potential survey
5. NACE TM 0109: Above ground survey technique for evaluating coating condition of underground pipeline
6. DNV RP F101: Guidelines for corroded pipeline
7. DNVGL-RP-F116: Integrity management of submarine pipeline systems
8. NACE TM 0497: Measurement techniques related to criteria for cathodic protection of underground pipeline
9. NACE SP 0169: Control of external corrosion on underground or submerged metallic piping system

10. NACE TM 0106: Detection, testing and evaluation of microbiologically influenced corrosion (MIC) on external surfaces of underground pipeline

11. NACE SP 0102: Inline inspection of pipelines

12. NACE SP 502: Pipeline External Corrosion Direct Assessment

13. NACE SP 0204: Stress Corrosion Cracking Direct Assessment

14. NACE SP 0206: Internal Corrosion Direct Assessment for pipelines carrying dry gas

15. NACE SP 0106-2006: Control of internal corrosion in steel pipelines and piping

16. NACE SP 0110-2010: Wet gas Internal Corrosion Direct Assessment

17. Pipeline Risk Management manual

1.5: Terminology:

ACVG: Alternating current voltage gradient
CP: Cathodic protection
CIPL: Close interval potential logging
CAT: Current attenuation test

Direct Inspection: Physical examination of coating defect or corrosion activity

Disbandment: Loss of adhesion between a pipeline surface and protective coating due to adhesive failure, poor surface preparation, mechanical damage or excess of hydrogen evolution

DCVG: Direct current voltage gradient
ECDA: External corrosion direct assessment
Holiday: A discontinuity in the coating exposing unprotected surface to environment
Indirect Inspection: Survey or measurement of coating defect or corrosion activity on the above ground surface of pipeline. Ex CIPL, CAT & DCVG

ICDA: Internal corrosion direct assessment
ILI: Inline inspection
MAOP: Maximum allowable operating pressure
MIC: Microbiological influenced corrosion
PSP: Pipe to soil potential
Polarization: Change in corrosion potential of a structure due to current flow across structure/electrolyte interface

1.6 : Integrity management process flow diagram:

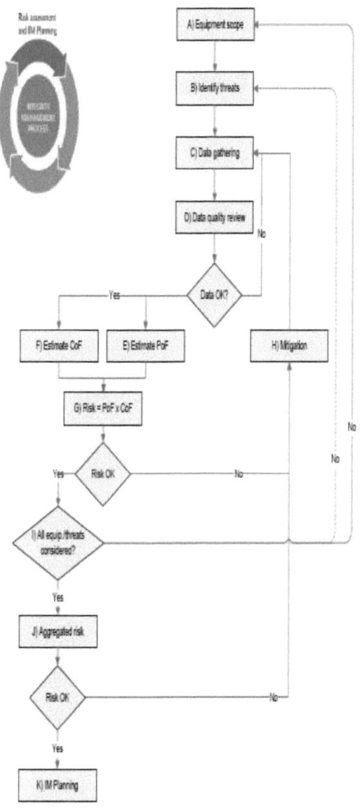

Risk assessment and IM Planning – main tasks and link to code requirements:

- Define equipment/item scope (i.e. all equipment/item that can lead to a failure)
- For each equipment/item, identify all threats which can lead to a failure
- For each threat; estimate risk
  - Consequence of failure (CoF)
  - Probability of failure (PoF)
- Propose plans for:
  - Inspection, monitoring and testing (IMT)
  - Mitigation, intervention and repair (MIR)
  - Integrity assessment (IA)

Fig 1 Integrity management process flow diagram

Chapter 2

Threats to pipeline integrity and threat analysis

2.1 Threats to pipeline integrity:

a) Time dependent:

i External corrosion

ii Internal corrosion

iii Stress corrosion cracking

b) Stable:

i Manufacturing defect

ii Welding and fabrication defect

iii Equipment and component failure: Gasket failure

c) Time independent:

i Third party damage

ii Vandalism: Sabotage

iii Incorrect operation

iv Weather related: Earthquake, lightening, floods

2.2 Potential threat analysis:

The table below gives potential threat analysis.

Table 1

Segment	Sl No	Risk description	Desirable practice/control	Action plan
External corrosion	1	Lack of proper selection of materials and coating, poor application of coatings, welding defects and inadequate CP may lead to pre-mature failure of pipeline	Proper selection of materials and coatings, proper application of coatings, minimizing welding defects and adequate cathodic protection	Quality control in fabrication and laying, Holiday testing, coating surveys, CP monitoring, thickness measurement, repair and refurbishment
Internal corrosion	2	Lapses in cleaning and drying of pipeline by pigging, lack of monitoring of oil or gas composition such as Co2, H2S and H2O, not injecting	Regular cleaning and drying of pipeline by pigging, monitoring of oil or gas composition for presence of H2O, Co2 and H2S, injection of corrosion	Carrying out cleaning of pipeline as per schedule, pig residue analysis, testing of oil or gas for knowing its constituents, removal of

		corrosion inhibitor, not doing ILI and corrosion monitoring	inhibitor if required, carrying out ILI and corrosion monitoring	water, Co2 and H2S, direct inspection such as UT or LRUT, Repair and refurbishment
Stress Corrosion Cracking	3	Absence of SCC testing and monitoring	Indirect and direct inspection though SCC tools, pressure testing, dig verification and NDT methods	Adherence to schedule for SCC inspection both indirect and direct, monitoring of pressure variation and repair and refurbishment
Manufacturing and Fabrication defects	4	Seam weld and girth weld defects, geometrical anomalies, and mechanical defects	Quality control checks in seam and girth welding, EGP before commissioning, NDT	PQT and WPQ, NDT and DT, Repair, and refurbishment

Equipment and component failure	5	Improper selection of equipment and components, faulty installation and misalignment, lack of proper operation, inspection, monitoring and maintenance and timely corrective action may lead to stresses on pipelines and pre mature failure	Procurement of equipment's and components as per standard specifications and testing certificates by approved agency, quality control in installation and testing, timely calibration, and functional testing, following SOP's, Monitoring and scheduled maintenance	Controlling mechanism such as internal and external audit should be in place to monitor proper inspection, operation, and maintenance practices as per SOP's. Scheduled Calibration and testing record should be maintained

Third party damage/ Vandalism	6	Lack of identification of vulnerable areas and its regular patrolling, awareness program for residents near pipelines and controlling measures for pipe failure and arresting leak may result into pre mature pipeline failure	System of Regular foot patrolling and helicopter surveillance and awareness program for nearby residents should be in place. Warning signs should be in place. leak detection system should be in place.	24X7 Pipeline surveillance through guards and contact program with residents near pipeline should be followed. Leak detection system should be tested as per schedule. Mock drill should be done
Weather and earth related	7	Natural calamities such as earthquake, heavy rains and flood, landslide, storm, meandering of river, lightening	The protective measures should be taken for natural calamities such as sufficient depth of cover on land	Schedule monitoring of vulnerable locations at river crossing and steep slope may be done regularly

		etc may affect pipeline safety and integrity due to developed stresses on the pipe, wash out, exposure, crack or bend and failure.	and river bed, bank protection by stone pitching in wire mesh, HDD in critical areas like major river and creek and earthing of pipe through polarization cell and zinc anode. Regular patrolling of pipeline on land and river/creek should be done.	followed by taking corrective measures if required. Offsite drill for disaster managemen t should be done along with district authorities

Mechanical damage Pitting corrosion

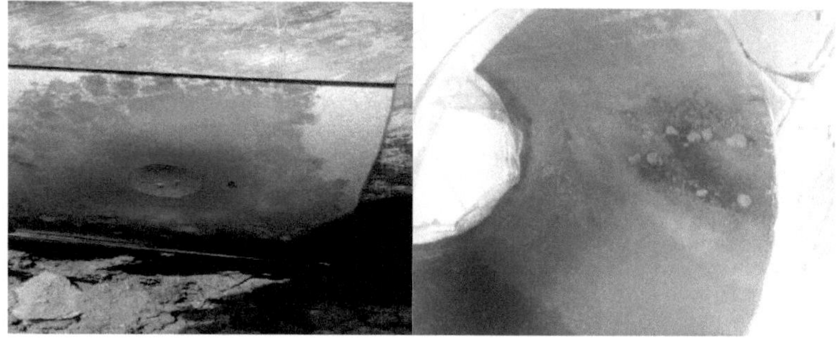

AC corrosion internal corrosion

Figure 2 Threats of corrosion and mechanical defect on integrity

Chapter 3

Risk Assessment

3.1 Consequence due to failure:

Potential impact area due to natural gas pipeline failure can be calculated by calculating radius of impact area

$r = 0.69 * d\sqrt{p}$

Where d = Outside diameter of pipeline in inch

p = MAOP of section of pipeline in psig

r = Radius of impact circle in feet

Or $r = 0.00315 * d\sqrt{p}$

Where d = Outside diameter of pipeline in mm

p = MAOP of section of pipeline in KPa

r = Radius of impact circle in meter

Thus, the radius of impact is more if diameter of pipeline and MAOP of the segment are more.

Impact is also more if the following is more:

a. Population density Ex City area

b. Environment damage such as forest, river or green area

c. Fire and explosion hazards due to domestic, commercial and industrial area

d. Importance of gas supply for example for transport or cooking purpose

3.2 Risk Assessment:

3.2.1 What is Risk?

Risk is described as product of two primary factors: The likelihood of failure or probability of failure and consequences or impact of failure.

3.2.2 Risk calculation of threat:

$Risk_i = P_i * C_i$ for a single threat

Total Risk for threats 1 to n will be equal to

$$\sum_{i=1}^{n} (P_i * C_i) \text{ for threat } i= 1 \text{ to } n$$

Total Risk = $P_1 * C_1 + P_2 * C_2 +\ldots\ldots\ldots+ Pn * Cn$

Where P is likelihood of failure and C is consequence of failure

1 to 9 is threat category as described in table 1

3.3 Objectives of Risk Assessment:

1. Prioritization of pipeline and its segments for scheduled integrity assessment and mitigating actions
2. Assessment of the benefits due to mitigating action
3. Determination of the most effective measures for the identified threats
4. Assessment of the integrity impact from inspection intervals
5. Assessment of the need for alternative inspection methodologies
6. Allocation of resources for more effective inspection methodologies and mitigation measures

7. Effective decision making for cost optimization by selecting appropriate inspection methodologies and mitigating measures

8. Planning qualified and experienced personnel for interpreting results and implementing mitigation measures

3.4 Data requirement for Risk Assessment:

Design

Pipe wall thickness, material and class, diameter, corrosion allowance, Soil resistivity and soil chemical analysis, Design pressure, operating pressure and MAOP

Manufacturing

Manufacturing process such as ERW, LSAW, HSAW etc, Type of coating, external and internal, Coating thickness, Hydro test pressure,

Construction

Year of construction, Type of joint coating, Hydro test pressure, Depth of cover, Cathodic protection details, EGP report

Operation and maintenance

Gas or liquid analysis Report, Pig residue report, Microbial analysis report, Flow conditions such as pressure, temperature, flow rate, O&M Manuals and SOP's, Leak/failure history and repair record, Corrosion rate by corrosion monitoring, ERDMP

Inspection

CP monitoring reports, CIPL, CAT and DCVG/ACVG survey reports, ILI Reports, Pressure test, ECDA & ICDA, Bell hole inspection and UT measurement report, Audit report

3.5 Classification of safety class for determining impact:

Table 2

Safety class	Classification of fluid		Classification of location		Examples/Impact
	petroleum products	NG, LPG,LNG	No frequent human activity	Frequent human activity	
Low			yes		Water line
Medium	yes	yes	yes		Onshore pipeline in rural areas and offshore, Platform
High	yes	yes		yes	Oil/Gas Terminal and compressor areas. Pipeline in urban areas.

3.6 Assigning probabilities or likelihood of failures:

Table 3

High (Probable)	Likelihood of failure is very high that is frequency is several times. The probability is high due to lack of any or all control measures for mitigating that threat or risk

Moderate (Possible)	Likelihood of failure is moderate that is frequency is one or two times in a year. This is due to effective control but need review for modification or better control
Low (Remote)	The possibility of failure is remote as all control measures are in place and no failure has occurred in past

3.7 Assigning impact or consequence of failure:

Table 4

High	Significant impact on the cost of production and loss of brand image due to leak and failure, repair and replacement, effects on public safety and environment, non-compliance of legal and regulatory requirements, legal proceedings. (For example, gas pipeline leak and fire in KG Basin and oil depot fire in India. Mostly in high safety class due to failure of control mechanism
Moderate	Moderate impact on cost of production due to leak and failure loss and repair and replacement. A little impact on brand image, public safety and environment. No serious legal or regulatory offences. Failure is not severe and can be controlled within less time. Ex leak between major and minor (Not reported). Mostly in medium safety class where control mechanism exists but need review
Low	Negligible impact on cost due to failure and also very negligible impact on brand image as well as effect on safety and environmental issues. No legal or regulatory offences. Ex minor leak (Not reported). Mostly in low safety class with all control

	mechanism in place

3.8 Risk matrix table:

Table 5

	Impact		
Probability	Low (1)	Moderate (2)	High (3)
Low (1)	Low (1)	Low (1)	Moderate (3)
Moderate (2)	Low (2)	Moderate (4)	High (6)
High (3)	Moderate (3)	High (6)	High (9)

3.9 Risk rating:

Table 6

Level of risk	Description	Rating (Impact * Likelihood
High	High risk is due to combination of moderate probability and high impact or high probability and moderate or high impact. Need priority to control probability to make it low as impact is not controllable	6 & 9
Moderate	Moderate risk is due to a combination of low probability with high impact, moderate probability with moderate impact and high probability with low impact. Need priority to control both moderate and	3 & 4

	high probability to low	
Low	Low risk is due to a combination of low probability with low and moderate impact and moderate probability with low impact. Since either probability or impact is low hence risk is minimal. However moderate probability should be controlled to low	1 & 2

3.10 What does the risk matrix say?

- Probability of failure is major indication which is directly related to lack of controlling measures in mitigating threats causing failures and incurring repair and replacement cost. The identification of threats and its controlling practice is important for reducing probability of failure.

- Impact of failure is time dependent. The severity of impact depends upon external factors which are not under control. The population density and geographical conditions of the surrounding are such factors. These factors will increase with the time only.

- As it is said that “Prevention is better than cure” so probability can be reduced from high and moderate to low by effective controlling mechanism for anticipated threats. As probability becomes low so even impact is moderate or high, risk of failure is moderate. Impact can also be minimized by controlling post leak hazards such as plugging the leak and extinguishing the fire post failure.

3.11 Examples:

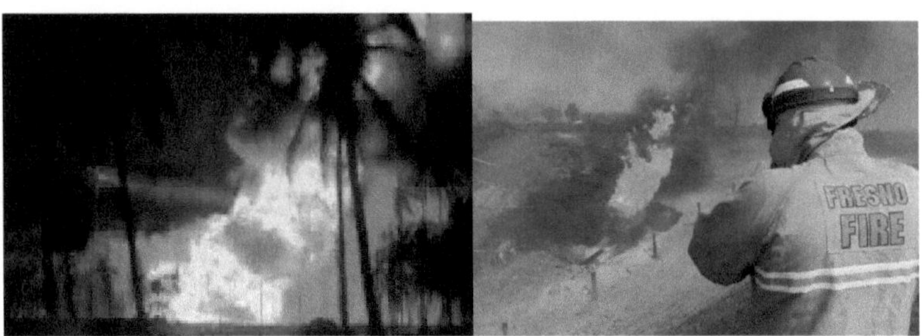

Explosion in gas pipeline in KG Basin and California

Fire in gas pipeline in Delhi   Fire in Mexico oil pipeline

Figure 3

3.12 Comparison of risk assessment and risk management plan:

Table 7

Sl No	Incident	Segment	Prob	Imp	Risk Rating	Risk Management Plan
1	Explosion in Gas pipeline in KG Basin	Internal corrosion due to presence of water, H2S, Co2 in gas	High	High	High	Dehydration and desulphurization of gas, cleaning by pigging, corrosion monitoring, ILI, Repair and/or replacement
2	Explosion in Gas pipeline in California	Third party damage due to lack of patrolling and control of leak	High	High	High	Regular patrolling and leak monitoring, arresting of leak and repair. Immediate fire extinguishing
3	Fire in gas pipeline in Delhi	Third party damage due to lack of patrollin	High	High	High	Regular patrolling and leak monitoring, arresting of leak and

		g and control of leak				repair. Immediate fire extinguishing
4	Gasoline fuel fire in Mexico oil line	Third party damage due to lack of patrolling and control of leak	High	High	High	Regular patrolling and leak monitoring, arresting of leak and repair. Immediate fire extinguishing

Chapter 4

Integrity Assessment

4.1 Objectives of Integrity assessment:

1. Based on the risk assessment of different threats at different segments and determining risk level, selection of proper tools for integrity assessment.

2. Based on the results of integrity assessment tools, selection of mitigation, intervention, and repair methodology.

3. Review of selection of integrity assessment tools and mitigation, intervention, and repair methodology.

4. Cost optimization in the selection of proper integrity assessment tools and mitigation methodology

5. Assessing requirement of qualified and experienced personnel for implementing integrity assessment tools and analysis of its results

4.2 Integrity Assessment Tools and its Frequency:

Table 8

Sl No	Threats	Integrity Assessment Tools		Frequency	
		Pigging line	Non pigging line	Pigging line	Non pigging line
		Feed quality Analysis for presence of Co_2, H_2S, H_2O, SO_2, condensate, pH, chlorine		Once in a year for onshore and twice in a year. Frequency may be earlier based on gas quality	

		Muck analysis for detecting Fe, Sulfate, H_2O, pH, Sulfur, SRB	N/A	After each de-scaling	N/A
		Scrapper pigging	N/A	Dry gas once in 5 years Wet gas, LPG, and dedicated ATF once in a year Crude oil and ATF with other products once in 3 months Non-ATF products 6 months	N/A
		Internal corrosion monitoring by installing coupons, ER probes, LPR probes etc. Probes must be installed at 6 o clock position in a running stream at vulnerable		Continuous monitoring is required. Corrosion rate should be less than 1mpy. If more, then corrosion inhibitor should be injected. It should not be more than	

<table>
<tr><td rowspan="5">1</td><td rowspan="5">Internal corrosion</td><td colspan="2">locations</td><td colspan="2">5mpy
Corrosion coupons Once in six months
Corrosion probes Once in 3 months</td></tr>
<tr><td>In line inspection by suitable tools like MFL or others followed by bell hole inspection and pipe thickness measurement</td><td>N/A</td><td>Dry Natural gas once in 10 years
Wet Natural gas once in 5 years
Petroleum once in 5 years
UT measurement at platform and terminals once in 2 years</td><td>N/A</td></tr>
<tr><td colspan="2">Pressure testing at 1.25 times MAOP</td><td colspan="2">Once in five years</td></tr>
<tr><td colspan="2">ICDA</td><td colspan="2">Once in five years</td></tr>
<tr><td>N/A</td><td>IPS tools for</td><td>N/A</td><td>Platform and</td></tr>
</table>

			measuring wall thickness		terminal and onshore 2 years, offshore 5 years
		Visual inspection		five years for subsea, 1 year for splash zone, 2 years for platform & onshore line	
2	External corrosion	CP ON and OFF monitoring is done to maintain polarized potential (OFF) within -850 mV to -1200 mV for onshore pipeline. Continuous potential survey is done to measure on potential for offshore line for sacrificial anode system		Once in a year for onshore pipeline and once in five years for offshore pipelines.	
		Coating integrity survey CIPL, CAT and DCVG or ACVG for checking adequacy of CP system and integrity of coating followed by bell hole inspection , coating adhesion test and pipe thickness		Once in five years for onshore pipeline. ROV inspection is done for visual coating damage and anode condition once in five years for offshore pipeline. UT measurement at platform and	

		measurement		onshore 2 years, subsea five years	
		Soil testing for analysis of corrosiveness of soil like presence of microbes, pH value, moisture content, O_2, chlorine		Once in five years or as required if soil is contaminated by effluents	
		Pressure testing at 1.25 times MAOP		Once in five years	
		Inline inspection as in internal corrosion	IPS tool for measurement of wall thickness	As in Internal corrosion	Platform, terminal and onshore 2years, offshore 5 years
		ECDA		Once in five years	
3	Third party damage	Line patrolling of pipelines by company officials leak detection system check		once in a year once in a year	
4	Risk Assessment	Quantitative risk assessment to evaluate population density and safety class		Once in a five years	
5	Manufactu	Geometri	N/A	Once before	N/A

	ring and construction defects	c pigging is done before hydro testing and after cleaning to detect dents and other internal surface deviations		commissioning	
		NDT		Once in five years	
		Pressure testing at 1.25 times MAOP		Once in five years	
		On bottom stability, lateral displacement and free span survey for offshore pipeline		Once in five years	
6	O&M	Inspection and testing of leak detection system and safety valves		Once in six months	
		Inspection and testing of safety interlocks and communication system		Once in three months	
7	SCC	Detection of stress related cracks by SCC		Once in 10 years or 5 years as the case	

		tools	may be
8	Weather and environment related	Analysis of weather and environment related changes such as earthquake, lightening, flood	As and when required

Chapter 5
Inspection, monitoring and testing

5.1 Inspection, monitoring and testing tools for threat detection

Table 9

Detection tools	**External Corrosion**	**Internal Corrosion**	**Third Party Damage**	**Incorrect Operation**	**Manufacturing**	**Construction**	**Weather Related**
Patrolling	No	No	Yes	No	No	No	Yes
Physical Inspection	Yes	No	Yes	No	Yes	Yes	Yes
CP monitoring	Yes	No	No	No	No	No	No
Coating survey	Yes	No	Yes	No	No	Yes	No
Internal Cleaning	No	Yes	No	No	No	No	No
ILI	Yes	Yes	Yes	No	Yes	Yes	No

NDT	Yes	Yes	Yes	No	Yes	Yes	No
EGP	No	No	No	No	Yes	Yes	No
Safety testing	No	No	No	Yes	No	No	No
SOP’s & Audit	Yes	Yes	Yes	Yes	No	No	Yes
WPQ	No	No	No	No	Yes	Yes	No
Pressure testing	Yes	Yes	Yes	No	Yes	Yes	No
ECDA	Yes	No	Yes	No	No	Yes	No
ICDA	No	Yes	No	No	No	No	No
Feed Analysis	No	Yes	No	No	No	No	No
Pig Residue Analysis	No	Yes	No	No	No	No	No
QRA	No	No	Yes	No	No	No	Yes
Soil testing	Yes	No	No	No	No	No	Yes

Corrosion monitoring	Yes	Yes	No	No	No	No	No
Leak testing	In case of leak due to various reasons						
Seismic Survey	No	No	No	No	No	No	Yes

Chapter 6

Inspection tools technology

6.1 The various inspection tools technology is available as below:

1. Deformation:

i Caliper (Single and multi-channel)

2. Metal loss:

i Magnetic flux leakage (MFL), Axial, radial and circumferential

ii UT (Ultrasonic wall thickness measurement), High resolution

iii Long range ultrasonic thickness (LRUT)

3. Cracks

i Ultrasonic crack detection (Axial and circumferential)

ii EMAT (Electromagnetic Acoustic Transducer)

1. **Deformation:** It is caused by stress and results into ovality, dent, wrinkles and cracks weakening pipe strength.

Caliper (Single and multi-channel)

Caliper pigging is Used for measuring inside diameter and geographical anomalies. Odometer wheels generate the distance data and sensors record the inside diameter. The data is recorded in a digital recorder in the tool. A locator mounted on the tool indicates location of the caliper pig. A multi-channel caliper pig can measure different data simultaneously.

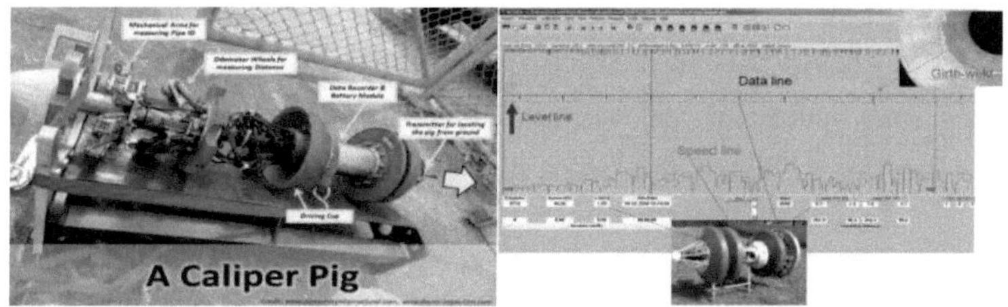

Figure 4 A caliper tools (Single and multi-channel for measuring inside diameter

2.0 Metal loss

i Magnetic flux leakage (MFL), Axial and circumferential

MFL is an electromagnetic tool used for measuring metal loss and other anomalies such as dent or crack. Metal loss anomalies can be prioritized for dig verification and repair or replacement. The principle of operation is based on electromagnetic principle. A powerful magnet magnetizes the steel pipe. Magnetic flux leaks at the defect. The leakage flux is collected by detectors placed between two poles of the magnet. Sensors measure anomalies in both axial and circumferential direction if circumferential and axial MFL tools are used.

Figure 5 MFL tool for detection and measurement of metal loss

ii UT (Ultrasonic wall thickness measurement), High resolution

Ultrasonic wall thickness measurement is done through ultrasonic waves which are generated by transducers and ultrasonic waves are received by receiver. The time taken for travel of sound waves to material and back is calculated through echo and velocity of sound is programmed. Thickness is calculated based on time taken and velocity of sound.

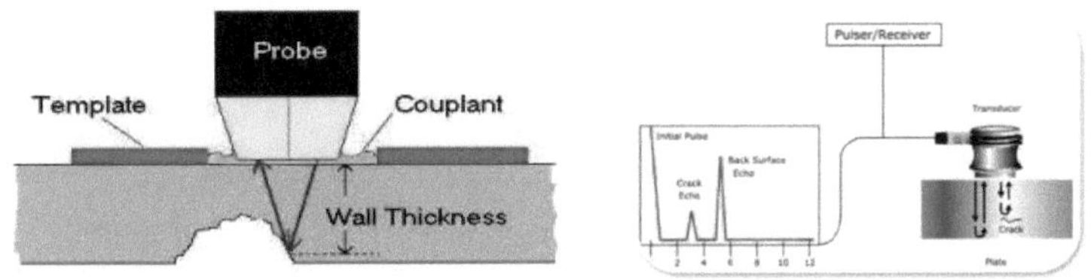

Figure 6 Ultrasonic thickness measurement devices

iii Long range ultrasonic thickness (LRUT)

Long range or guided wave ultrasonic thickness measurement is done on ultrasonic wave theory. This method needs no couplant for contact between probe and surface and also this can be done from single test point. Here also, transducers transmit sound waves which are guided through pipe wall and reflected sound waves are collected by receiver and recorded in graphical form.

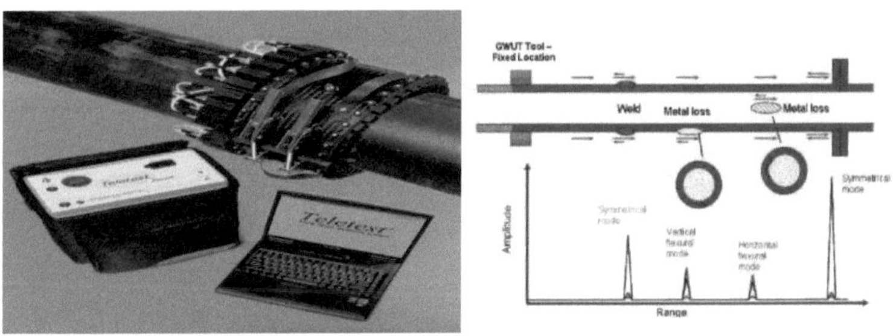

Figure 7 LRUT for measurement of wall thickness from one location

3.Cracks

i Ultrasonic crack detection Axial and circumferential:

Based on the principle of ultrasonic wave theory, crack can be detected and measured through ultrasonic meter with flaw detector at a defined frequency.

ii EMAT (Electromagnetic Acoustic Transducer):

EMAT transducer consists of a socket, induction coil and permanent magnet. Magnet produces a magnetic field. An alternating current is fed into the induction coil and Eddy current is produced by electromagnetic oscillations. Eddy current interferes with the permanent magnetic field creating ultrasonic waves directly on the surface of the pipeline. The advantage is the use of this technique without couplant. Also, EMAT gives accurate measurement.

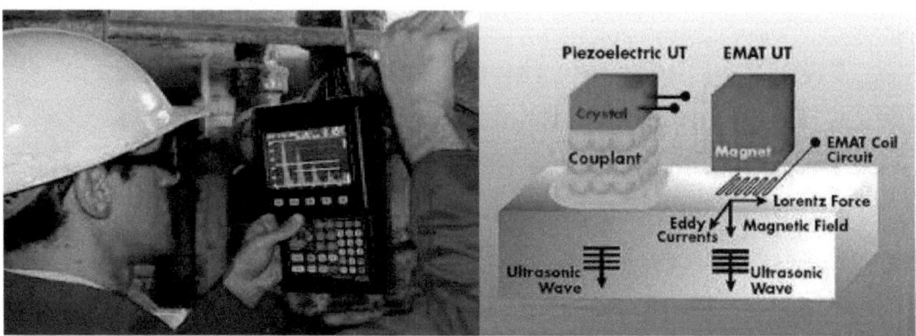

Figure 8 EMAT technologies for measurement of thickness and crack

4.0 Selection of inspection technology based on nature of anomalies

Table 10

Sl No	Nature of anomalies	Tools				
		MFL	**UT**	**LRUT**	**Caliper**	**EMAT**
1	Metal loss (External)	Yes	Yes	Yes	No	Yes
2	Metal loss (Internal)	Yes	Yes	No	No	No
3	Cracks all types	No	Yes	No	No	Yes
4	Deformation such as Dent, ovality, wrinkles & cracks	No	No	No	Yes	No

Chapter 7

Inline Inspection through intelligent pigging

What is intelligent pigging?

Intelligent pigging can be defined as the pigging that generates and records some data for analysis for establishing the health of the pipeline segment in quantifiable terms.

Objective of the inline inspection:

Following are the objectives:

- ❖ To determine if any defect detected by the inline inspection would fail at the rerated pressure.
- ❖ To determine if any existing defect can extend and cause failure at the rerated pressure.
- ❖ To consider all other factors (e.g. cracks, extensive fracture propagation) which could conceivably influence the integrity of the pipeline at the rerated pressure?

Types of intelligent pigging:

1. Geometrical pigging
2. Corrosion monitoring

Corrosion monitoring can be further classified based on principle of MFL and ultrasonic. MFL inspection tool is further classified as conventional, high resolution and transverse field.

Pre-requisites for intelligent pigging:

Pipeline design should follow certain norms to facilitate intelligent pigging:

- Be perfectly straight from end to end
- Have a constant ID with no weld penetration
- Be perfectly round
- Have an inside surface which is polished or epoxy coated
- Have no off-takes

- Contain no valves or any other device
- Be pumping a product at a speed of about 1m/sec.
- Should be equipped with suitably designed pig Launchers/ Receivers to launch and receive pig.

Types of anomalies:

The different anomalies in a pipeline which may affect integrity of a pipeline are as follows:

- Metal Loss (corrosion and gouges)
- Metallurgical (hard spots, inclusions, laminations, and weld porosity)
- Cracks (axial)
- Cracks (circumferential)
- Dents and buckles with or without metal loss

Defining anomalies:

- **Imperfection:**

This may cause failure above the pressure that causes nominal yield of the pipe.

- **Defect:**

This will fail at or below the pressure that causes nominal yield of the pipe.

- **Critical Defect:**

This will fail at or below the maximum allowable operating pressure

Facilities for intelligent pigging: Pig launcher and receiver

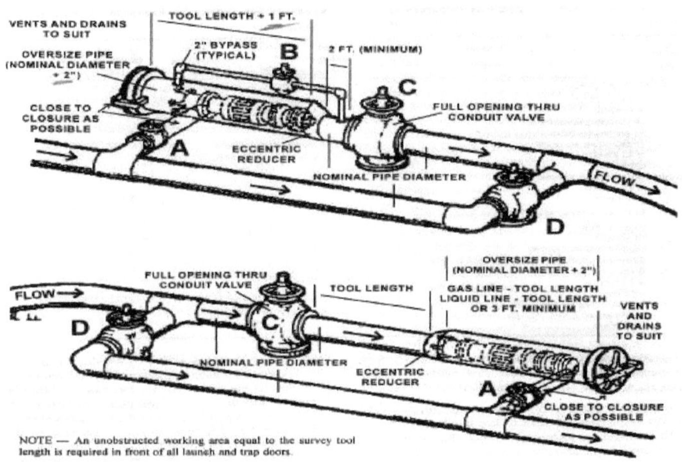

Method of defining severity of a metal loss anomaly:

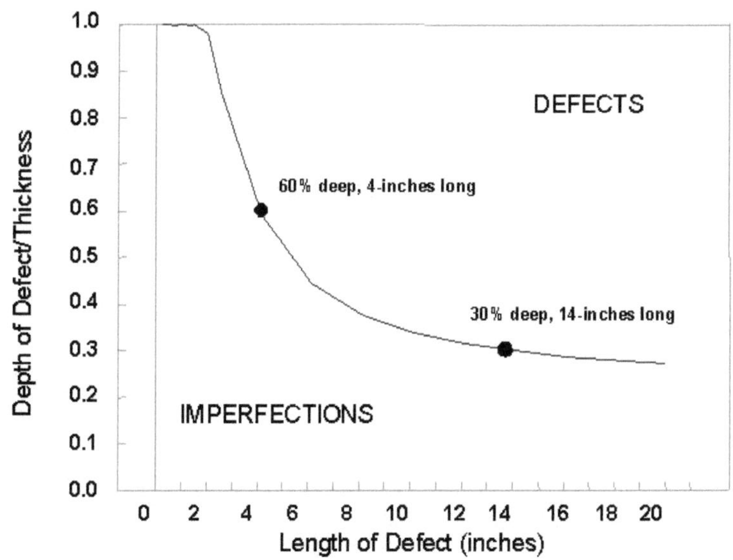

MFL and Ultrasonic Inspection tool:

Basic Principle of Magnetic Flux Leakage Tool:

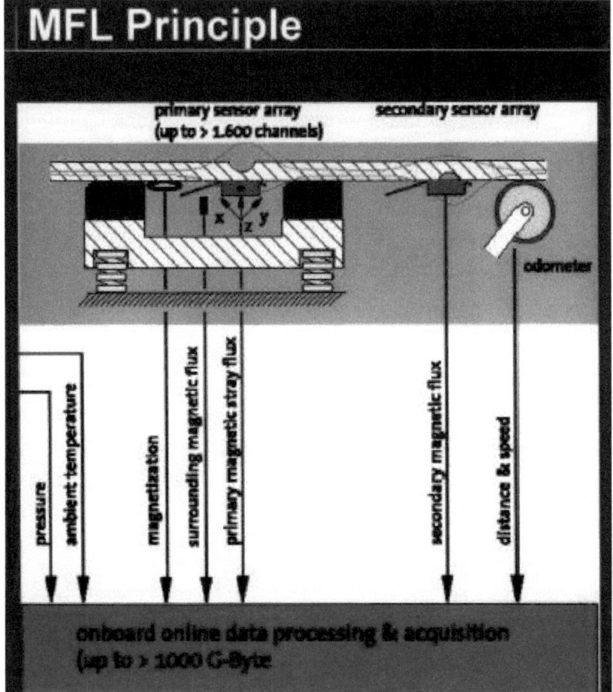

Magnetic flux leakage tool

Basic Principle of Ultrasonic Tool:

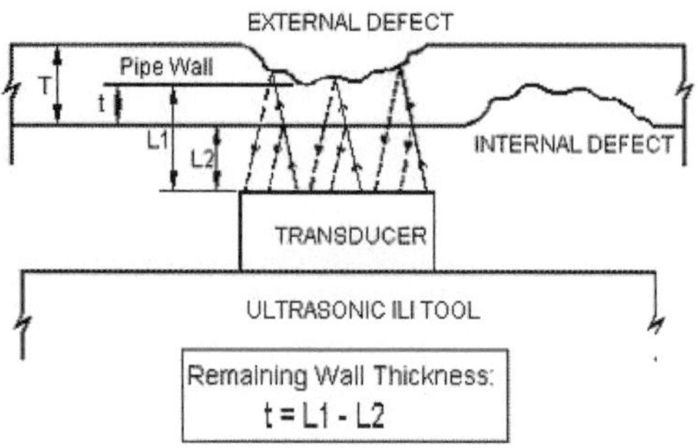

Ultrasonic tool

Chapter 7

External Corrosion Direct Assessment

7.1 Standards:

ASME B 31.8S:

A structured process for establishing the integrity of underground pipelines.

NACE SP 0502:

A four-step process to evaluate the impact of external corrosion on the integrity of a pipeline.

7.2 Benefits:

1. A continuous process that proactively seeks to prevent external corrosion defects from growing to a size that could impact structural integrity.
2. Provides the advantage and benefit of locating areas where defects can form in the future rather than only areas where defects have already formed.
3. Primary purpose of ECDA is to identify location of future external corrosion and take preventive actions
4. External corrosion is a threat to pipeline integrity and its baseline is established to correlate with future trend
5. ECDA has limitations so far as its applicable tools are concerned. For example, poorly coated or bare pipelines coating integrity surveys does not give accurate holidays and thus probable corrosion defects
6. ECDA should be applied in totality and not in parts. Any analysis in part may not give accurate results and decision may be inappropriate.
7. ECDA is technology driven tool and specialists are required to use the tool and interpret its results. Any discrepancy in data analysis may lead to inappropriate decision

7.3 The four steps required for effective evaluation:

7.3.1 Pre-assessment:

The objective of the pre-assessment is to study feasibility of carrying out ECDA, select indirect tools and identify ECDA regions.

Approach is data collection related to pipe specifications, construction details, external corrosion, soil and environment around pipeline, operation and maintenance practices and monitoring, inspection and repair records.

7.3.2 Indirect inspection:

The objective is to identify and define the severity of coating faults, other anomalies such as short cased crossing, interference, inadequate cathodic protection and areas prone to corrosion activity that have occurred or occurring.

Two or more indirect inspection tools are applied on the whole segment of pipe to detect corrosion anomalies under wide variety of conditions

7.3.3 Direct inspection:

The objective is to analyze indirect inspection data and identify sites of corrosion activity and verify physically defects and corrosion activity identified from indirect inspection

The approach is as follows:

i Excavation of the identified areas susceptible to corrosion activity and data collection
ii Measurement of coating defect and corrosion defect
iii Prioritization of the defects found by the inspection tools whether minor, moderate or severe

iv Evaluation of coating performance
v Analysis of corrosion activity
vi Prevention, mitigation, and repairs

7.3.4: Post assessment:

The objective is to analyze the data from pre-assessment, indirect inspection and direct inspection and overall assess the effectiveness of the ECDA process, reprioritize indications and determine reassessment intervals.

The approach is root cause analysis and mitigation and repair

7.4 Pre-assessment:

7.4.1: Data collection:

The following data is collected:

Pipe specifications:

Pipe material and grade, diameter, wall thickness, year of commissioning, manufacturing process

Construction related:

Route map, As built drawings, pipe book, alignment sheet, P&I diagrams, pipe cover, HDD drawings, cased crossing, river and rail crossing drawings

Soil/environment:

Soil resistivity and chemical analysis record, drainage and compaction report, topography, environmental conditions, weather related

Operational:

MAOP, MOP, operating temperature, monitoring reports, surveillance and inspection reports, repair/replacement history, leak and rupture history due to external corrosion, history of

MIC, third party damage, hydro testing reports, ILI, ECDA, CIPL, DCVG and CAT survey report

Corrosion control:

Details of CP system, CP monitoring reports, Coating type, coating condition and repair history, CP current density, Dig verification report, ER probes monitoring, Interference survey reports, UT measurement report

7.4.2: Assessment of ECDA feasibility:

Feasibility analysis is done to analyze data for determining whether indirect inspection tools can be applied for ECDA or ECDA is not feasible for certain locations. Application of ECDA is difficult at the following locations.

i where coating disbandment takes place as CP current does not reach the pipeline under disbanded coating

ii Pipeline surrounded by rocky materials as CP current does not reach pipe surface

iii Pipeline under concrete and pavement

iv Frozen ground where CP current requirement is very high

v Interference prone areas such as other pipelines in the vicinity, AC transmission lines, DC traction railways etc

vi Cased road and railway crossings

vii Inaccessible or non-approachable areas

In case proven indirect inspection tools cannot be applied on certain locations then based on history of defects and repair, direct inspection tools may be employed.

7.4.3: Selection of indirect inspection tools:

The selection of indirect assessment tools is an important part of pre-assessment. Minimum two tools are selected based on the data available and type of locations where results are dependable and match with the direct assessment.

The purpose of selecting two tools is this that strength of one tool compensates the limitations of other.

Table 11

Locations	CIPL	CAT	DCVG or ACVG
Coating holidays	Large	Small and large	Small and large
Near River or water crossing	Large	Large	Large
Frozen ground	Not possible	Small and large	Not possible
Stray current interference	Large	Small and large	Small and large
Disbanded coating	Not possible	Not possible	Not possible
Under AC transmission line	Large	Large	Small and large
Under paved roads	Not possible	Small and large	Not possible
Cased crossings	Not possible	Not possible	Not possible
Deep burial	Not possible	Not possible	Not possible
Marshy area	Large	Small and large	Small and large
Rocky terrain	Not possible	Large	Not possible

Inference drawn:

1. No indirect inspection tool is applicable for location of coating disbandment, cased crossing and deep buried pipeline
2. The choices are to select two tools which complement each other, depending upon their strength and limitations.

Table 12

Conditions	Combinations of two tools
Coating holidays	CAT and ACVG or DCVG/CIPL and DCVG or ACVG
Near river or water crossing	As above
Under frozen conditions	CAT only
Stray current interference	CAT and ACVG or DCVG/CIPL and DCVG or ACVG
Under AC transmission line	CIPL or CAT and DCVG or ACVG
Under paved road	CAT only
Marshy area	CIPL or CAT and DCVG or ACVG
Rocky area	CAT only

7.4.4: Identification of ECDA regions:

ECDA regions are identified on the basis of similar physical characteristics where similar indirect inspection tools are employed.

The identification of ECDA regions help in the selection of indirect inspection tools with the aim of achieving good result and also for economic reasons.

Table 13

Pipeline characteristics and physical conditions	CIPL and ACVG/DCVG	CAT and ACVG/DCVG	CAT only
Coated pipelines in all soil types, interference zone areas due to pipeline, AC line or DC traction and near river crossing	Can be done	Can be done	Not applicable
Frozen condition, under paved roads and rocky areas	Not possible	Not possible	Can be done
Coating disbandment, cased crossing and deep buried pipeline	Not possible	Not possible	Not possible

7.5: Indirect inspection:

7.5.1: Introduction

The objective of the indirect inspection is to identify and define the severity of coating faults and other anomalies at areas where corrosion activities may have occurred earlier or may occur in future.

7.5.2: Approach

i. At least two indirect inspection tools are applied at all segment of the pipeline as described in pre-assessment section.

ii. Data obtained from the two inspection tools is aligned and compared for correct assessment of the data.

iii. The indirect inspection tools are selected on the basis of its strength and limitations and hence, the segment areas and selected tools must complement each other.

iv. The data obtained will depend upon the right selection of indirect inspection tools and accurate measurement of the data

v. Finally, data interpretation is also important and is to be done by qualified and experienced CP engineers

7.5.3: Classification of severity of coating defects:

Table 14

Inspection tool	**Minor**	**Moderate**	**Severe**
CIPL	Small dips in ON and OFF potential and OFF potential above – 0.85 V	Medium dips in ON and OFF potential and OFF potential just above - 0.85 V	Large dips in ON and OFF potential and OFF potential below - 0.85 V
DCVG	% IR drop between 0 to 15	% IR drop is between 16 to 35	% IR drop is > 35
CAT and ACVG	signal loss is low up to 15 dB/Km	signal loss is moderate >15≤30 dB/Km	signal loss is very high >30 dB/Km

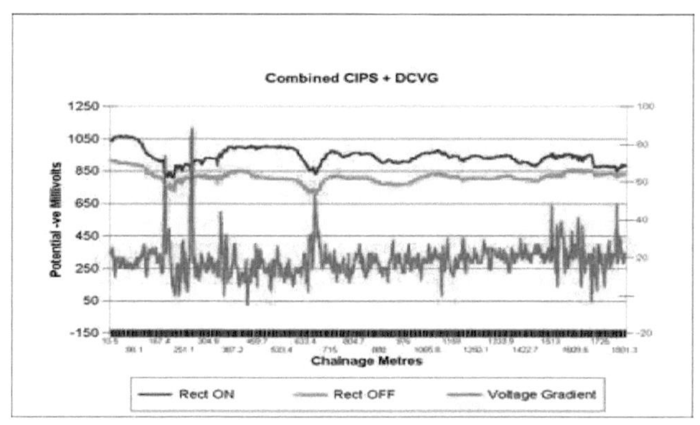

Figure 9 CIPL and DCVG survey graph

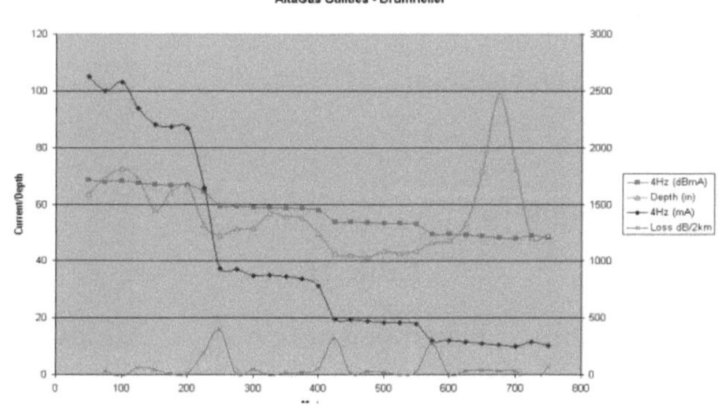

Figure 10 CAT graph

Figure 11 Coating defect

7.6: Direct examination:

7.6.1: Objective:

To verify physically defects and its severity and corrosion activity identified from indirect inspection.

7.6.2 : Approach:

Prioritization of the defects found by the inspection tools

Excavation of the identified areas susceptible to corrosion activity and data collection

Measurement of coating defect and corrosion defect

Evaluation of remaining strength that is severity of the corrosion

Analysis of corrosion activity

Process evaluation

7.6.3: Prioritization:

Table 15

Immediate action	Scheduled action	Monitoring
Severe indications in close vicinity	moderate indications in close vicinity	Individual minor indications in isolated areas
Group of moderate indications in close vicinity	Group of minor indications in close vicinity	
Moderate indications in regions of severe prior corrosion	Minor indications in regions of moderate prior corrosion	

7.6.4: Excavation and data collection:

The following steps are followed.

1. Before excavation is done, location should be verified by using GPS.
2. Excavation is required to be done in a long stretch if a cluster of severe or moderate defects are present.
3. The following data is recorded and test is carried out before excavation
   - i Pipe to soil potential measurement
   - ii Soil resistivity measurement
   - iii pH value of water table
   - iv Soil chemical analysis for SRB, salts, acids and other corrosive chemicals such as sulfates, bicarbonates and sulfides
4. Excavation is done as required and pipe is exposed.
5. Physical inspection is carried out for assessing nature of coating defect and corrosion activity on surface of pipeline
6. Photographic impression of physical inspection of coating shall be taken
7. Coating defect size shall be measured in length, width and depth.
8. Coating shall be removed and during the process, coating adhesion and coating disbandment shall be checked.
9. Pipe surface shall be cleaned thoroughly and all corrosion products shall be removed and collected for further lab analysis for detection of Fe2O3, Sulfur, SRB, H2O
10. NDT test such as UT and MPT should also be carried out for evaluating metal loss due to external or internal corrosion and any crack on the pipeline
11. Physical examination of type of corrosion and measurement of metal loss in length, width, and depth.
12. Photographic impression of coating disbandment and type of corrosion and its size shall be taken.

13. Any other measurement or testing required for analysis shall be done.

Figure 12 Coating disbandment and external corrosion

7.6.5: Remaining strength evaluation and remaining life calculation:

i Remaining strength evaluation is done by calculating critical failure pressure as per DNV-RP-F-101 considering depth and length of corrosion

ii The failure pressure should be more than 1.1* MAOP, then pipeline is safe. If failure pressure is less than 1.1* MAOP, then immediate rectification measures are required.

iii Remaining life can be calculated by arriving at rate of corrosion in mmpy and time taken to reach failure pressure at same corrosion rate. If corrosion rate is more, then failure may take place earlier than projected.

7.6.6: In process evaluation:

In process evaluation is done to compare criteria of indirect inspection and direct inspection. The criteria for immediate repair/replacement, schedule corrective action and monitoring shall be decided based on remaining strength evaluation.

7.7 Post assessment:

7.7.1 Objective:

The objective of post assessment is to define reassessment intervals, determine whether or not to reprioritize indications and overall assess the effectiveness of the ECDA process.

7.7.2 Approach:

The post assessment steps are followed as under:

1. Remaining life calculation
2. Root cause analysis
3. Mitigation
4. Reclassification and reprioritization
5. Determining reassessment intervals
6. Assessment of ECDA effectiveness
7. Feedback and continuous improvement

7.7.3: Reclassification and reprioritization:

Classification of defects as severe, scheduled and monitoring and prioritization in that order are done based on direct examination and strength and residual life assessment.

Based on the result and prior experience, reclassification and reprioritization can be done if there is a variation in classification and/or priority between direct examination and result.

7.7.4: Reassessment interval:

Reassessment interval is decided on the basis of residual life assessment. It is half of the residual life. For example, if residual life is 10 years, then reassessment shall be done in five years.

7.7.5: Assessment of ECDA effectiveness:

The process followed in ECDA is reviewed from pre assessment level to direct examination whether objective is fulfilled. The data on indirect inspection and direct examination should match each other and results should not differ. If results differ or defects are over looked then revisit of ECDA is required.

7.7.6: Feedback and continuous improvement:

Based on the review of effectiveness of ECDA, continuous improvement is required. This may require change of technology and tools for indirect inspection and direct examination, employing more trained field engineers, improving testing procedures and analyzing data correctly.

Based on the result and prior experience, reclassification and reprioritization can be done if there is a variation in classification and/or priority between direct examination and result.

7.7.8: ECDA records:

All the documents and records should be preserved from all the four steps namely pre assessment, indirect inspection, direct examination and post assessment.

The documents and records will be required during reassessment for comparison purpose. The effectiveness of ECDA will depend upon the previous interpretation and future results. That will decide requirement of reclassification and reprioritization.

Chapter 8

Internal Corrosion Direct Assessment

8.1: Standards:

SP0206-2006 – ICDA for Pipelines carrying Dry Natural Gas

SP0208-2008 – ICDA for Liquid Petroleum Pipelines

SP0110- 2010 – ICDA for wet gas Pipelines

8.2: Definition:

It is a four-step process to evaluate the impact of internal corrosion on the integrity of a pipeline.

8. Objective of internal corrosion direct assessment:

1. To enhance the assessment of internal corrosion in pipelines in order to ensure integrity
2. To carry out assessment of internal corrosion where conventional method such as ILI or pressure testing is not practical
3. To identify the locations vulnerable to internal corrosion due to accumulation of water

8.4: Four step process:

8.4.1: Pre-assessment:

8.4.1.1: Data collection:

1. Leak history
2. Mitigation measures
3. Pipeline details
4. Hydro test report,
5. Flow characteristics
6. Gas/Liquid analysis report(Presence of CO_2,O_2,H_2S,water)
7. ILI report
8. Debris analysis

9. Pipe material analysis,
10. Dig verification report,
11. NDT reports
12. Details of injection of corrosion inhibitor & biocides
13. Pipeline elevation profile
14. Corrosion rate
15. Operating conditions
16. Corrosion monitoring reports
17. internal coating

8.4.1.2 Feasibility study:

Data analysis and feasibility study for carrying out indirect inspection

8.4.1.3 Identification of ICDA regions:

Objective is Identifying ICDA regions due to pressure & temp variations.

8.4.2: Indirect inspection:

8.4.2.1: Identification of critical sites:

Those sites are susceptible to internal corrosion where water hold-up and accumulation of solids are possible. These are identified based on multi-phase flow modelling using available data to determine the Critical inclination angle of liquid holdup, pipeline inclination profile, corrosion rate model (severity of corrosion) and wall loss. Sag end in road, river, hill may be susceptible to water and liquid hold up.

8.4.2.2: Ranking of critical sites:

Critical sites are ranked that is priority of criticality is determined based on critical inclination angle and inclination profile.

8.4.3: Direct examination:

1. Critical site is excavated and pipe elevation is checked.

2. Coating is removed and thickness of pipe is measured by NDT

8.4.4 Post assessment:

1. Based on indirect and direct examination, residual strength and residual life assessment are carried out. Mitigation and repair are based on the residual strength and residual life assessment
2. Reassessment interval is based on residual life assessment.
3. Evaluation of effectiveness of ICDA is done based on the prediction by indirect inspection and its verification by direct examination. In case of any mismatch, ICDA process should be reviewed and may require modification.

Chapter 9

Internal corrosion

9.1: Factors responsible for internal corrosion:

1. Presence of corrosion constituents in gas or liquid such as water, H_2S, Co_2, O_2, basic sediments, Microorganisms
2. The presence of these constituents causes internal corrosion at the areas where chances of water accumulation is more that is at the bottom of inclines. A lower elevation and higher inclines will cause internal corrosion
3. Partial pressure of Co_2 more than 0.2 MPa and temperature more than 49 °C
4. Absence of scheduled cleaning pigging
5. Flow regime also causes corrosion. Stagnant or low flow less than 1 mps may cause internal corrosion. Between 1 to 10, rate is low and above 10 may cause erosion corrosion
6. Variation in pressure and temperature. Normally a higher temperature and pressure will cause more internal corrosion
7. Internal coating for flow effectiveness of piggable pipeline also causes internal corrosion due to coating damage

9.2: Gas and liquid quality specification for avoiding internal corrosion:

Table 16

Reference: Appendix A SP 0106- 2006

Constituents	Specifications
O2	Max 0.1 % mole
H_2S	Max 5.7 mg/m^3
Total S	Max 46 mg/m^3
Co_2	Max 2 % mole

Liquid condensate	Water vapor not to exceed 112 Kg/million³
Temperature	Between 4.4°C to 49°C
Basic sediment & water (BS&W)	Less than 0.5 % of the condensate

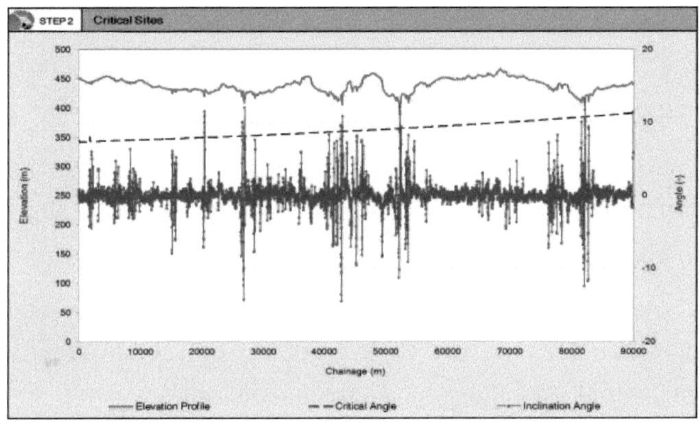

Fig 13 Elevation vs inclination

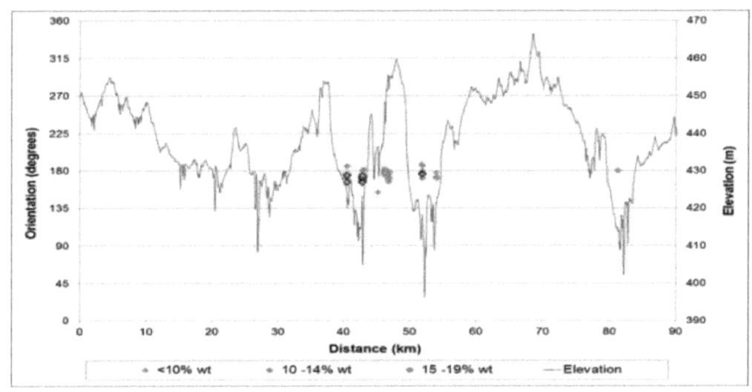

Fig 14 Wall loss at low elevation

Figure 13 shows that as inclination angles are more, elevation drops and chances of corrosion are more as accumulation of water and solid particles may be more.

Figure 14 shows that at low elevation, corrosion is detected mostly at 6 O clock positions.

Chapter 10

Corrosion monitoring

10.1 Salient points of corrosion monitoring:

1. Determination of critical zones on the basis of data gathered particularly elevation level and inclination angle where probability of accumulation of water, liquids and solids is more. As the elevation level drops, inclination angle is more and areas at 6 o clock position is vulnerable to internal corrosion

2. Measurement of wall thickness at areas of water accumulation by NDT methods. At least two methods should be employed.

3. Analysis of feed gas or liquid and muck after cleaning pigging for determination of quantity of corrosive constituents and microbial colonies and their role in causing internal corrosion. Moisture and H_2S are measured by moisture and H_2S analyzer for feed gas or liquid

4. ILI for identifying internal corrosion areas, depth of corrosion and types of corrosion.

5. Pressure testing for determination of pipe wall strength and any possible leak areas.

6. Corrosion monitoring by Coupons/ER probes/LPR probes at sites of water hold ups.

10.2: Monitoring selection method

Table 17

	Sweet wet gas	Sour wet gas	Sour crude oil/multiphase crude oil
General corrosion	Coupons LPR	Coupons LPR	Coupons LPR

	EN UT ER	EN UT	EN UT
Localized corrosion	Coupon EN UT	Coupon EN UT	Coupon EN UT
Environmentally Assisted cracking	H_2 Sensors	H_2 Sensors	H_2 Sensors
Flow assisted damage	Coupon ER EN	Coupon ER EN	Coupon ER EN

10.3: Corrosion Coupon Interpretations – NACE SP0775

Table 18

	Average corrosion rate		Maximum pitting rate	
	mm/y	mpy	mm/y	mpy
Low	< 0.025	< 1.0	< 0.13	< 5.0
Moderate	0.025 - 0.12	1.0 - 4.9	0.13 - 0.20	5.0 - 7.9
High	0.13 - 0.25	5.0 -10	0.21 - 0.38	8.0 - 15
Severe	>0.25	> 10	> 0.38	> 15

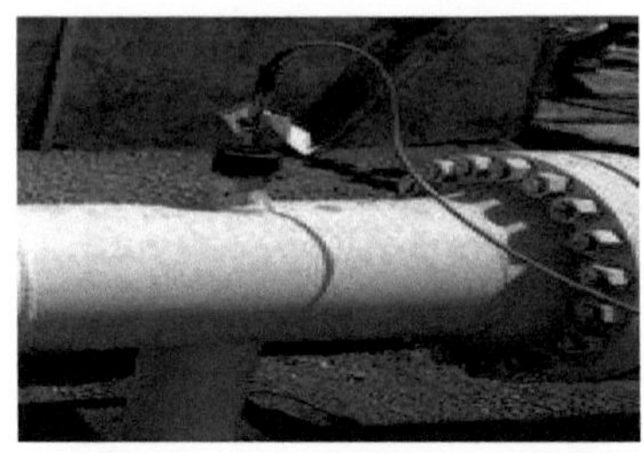
Figure 15 corrosion coupon

Figure 16 ER probe

Chapter 11

Fitness for purpose (FFP) and residual life assessment (RLA)

11.1 Partial safety factor and other coefficients:

Table 19

Safety class	**Partial safety factor**		
	Υm (Longitudinal corrosion factor)	Υd (Corrosion depth factor)	Ed (Fractile value)
Low	0.90	1.20	1.0
Medium	0.85	1.28	1.0
High	0.80	1.32	1.0

11.2: Fitness for purpose (FFP) and residual life assessment (RLA):

The critical pressure P_r as per DNV-RP-F-101

The equation is $P_r = \dfrac{[\Upsilon m * 2t * fu\ (1 - \Upsilon d(d/t)^*}{(D-t)\ \left(1 - \dfrac{\Upsilon d(d/t)^*)}{Q}\right.}$ Equation 1

$$(d/t)^* = (d/t)_{measured} + \varepsilon d * StD(d/t)$$

where d=depth of metal loss,

t is wall thickness of pipe

D is outside diameter

StD(d/t) is standard deviation of d/t ratio at 80 % confidence level and sizing accuracy of ± 0.10 which is .08

εd = Fractile value of corrosion depth

Υm = Partial safety factor (Longitudinal corrosion prediction)

ϒd = Partial safety factor (Corrosion depth)

fu = Tensile strength correcting factor based on temperature

fu = (SMTS-fu temp) *άu

SMTS is symmetrical mean tensile strength in N/mm2, fu temp is temperature factor and άu is material strength factor which is 0.96, fu temp is 0 for 50° C, 5 for 60° C and 15 for 75° C

$Q = \sqrt{1+0.31(l/\sqrt{D*t})^2}$, l is length of defect

For pipe to be safe, Pr should be more than 1.1*MAOP

Estimated repair factor = $\frac{1.1*MAOP}{Pr}$;

Should be less than 1

That is critical pressure should be more than 1.1* MAOP

Critical pressure is calculated at any time by putting metal loss values and length of metal loss. This will indicate whether pipeline is safe or not.

Corrosion rate Cr = $t-t_1/n$ where t and t_1 are original and latest remaining thickness in n years

The residual life can be calculated by projecting metal loss and length of metal loss and calculating critical pressure which should be equal to or near 1. The remaining life assessment graph from DNV RP F101 can assist in projecting metal loss and length.

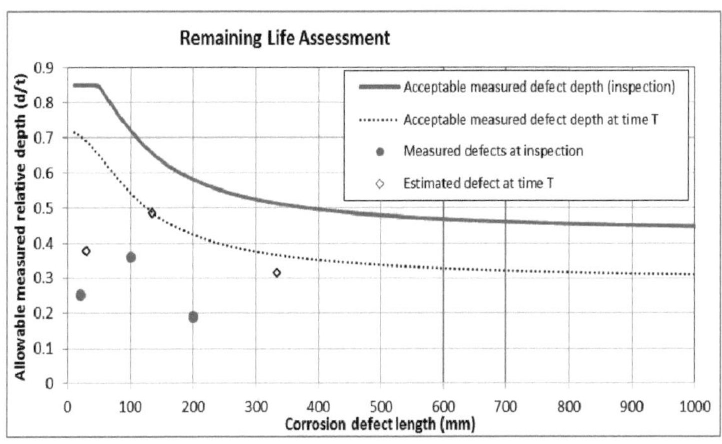

Ref DNV RP F101

11.3: Proposed action based on critical pressure:

Table 20

Integrity Finding	Response	Explanation	Proposed action
Severe	Immediate	Defect at failure point that is failure pressure less than 1.1 times MAOP	Immediate pressure reduction followed by repair or replacement
Moderate	Scheduled	Defect is significant but not at failure point such as failure pressure more than 1.1 times MAOP	Repair or replacement is scheduled before critical pressure is reached
Low	Monitoring	Defect is neither at failure point nor significant.	Preventive measures are required till next inspection

Chapter 12

Mitigation, intervention, and repair

Table 21

Sl No	Threat	Response	Proposed action
1	Weather related	Immediate	Pressure reduction/Repair/ Replacement
		Scheduled	Protection against washout and exposure
		Monitoring	Patrolling and visual inspection
2	Manufacturing related	Immediate	Repair by type B pressurized sleeve/Composite /Replacement
		Scheduled	Pressure reduction or Planned repair as above
		Monitoring	Pressure test and NDT
3	Construction related	Immediate	Repair by type B pressurized sleeve / Composite/Replacement
		Scheduled	Pressure reduction or Planned repair as above. Corrective action for stability and displacement
		Monitoring	Pressure test and NDT
4	External corrosion	Immediate	Pressure reduction/ Replacement/Repair by type B pressurized sleeve/type A reinforcing sleeve/ composite sleeve/ Mechanical leak clamp

		Schedule	Repair or replacement before the failure pressure reaches critical zone that is <1.1 times MAOP
		Monitoring	Regular monitoring as per integrity assessment plan
5	Internal corrosion	Immediate	Pressure reduction/Replacement/ Repair by type B pressurized sleeve
		Scheduled	Repair or replacement before the failure pressure reaches critical zone that is <1.1 times MAOP
		Monitoring	Regular monitoring as per integrity assessment plan

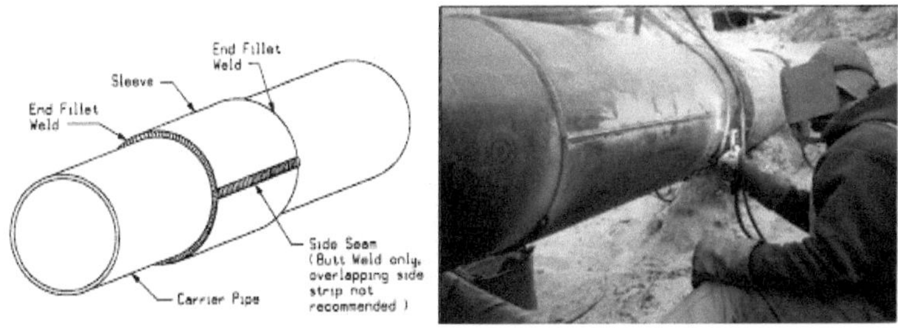

Split sleeve Welding in progress

Figure 17 Full circumferential split welded sleeve

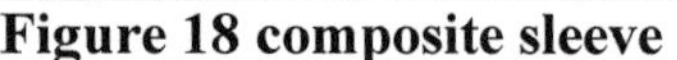

Figure 18 composite sleeve

Figure 19 Repair clamp

Chapter 13

Case studies on Integrity assessment

Case study 1:

The following is the pipeline particulars

Feed of the pipeline: Oil

Pipeline diameter: 355.6 mm

Pipeline thickness: 14.3 m

MAOP: 83 Kg/Cm2

Year of commissioning: 2008

Length of pipeline: 9 Km

Grade: API 5L X-60

Design temperature: 90° C

Inspection and testing data:

CP Parameters: PSP (OFF) within -0. 85 to – 1.2 V

CIPL & DCVG Survey indicating coating defects, not repaired

In line inspection (ILI) and SCC inspection: Not done

Internal corrosion monitoring by ER probe: 5 mpy

LRUT measurement at terminal: 14.2 mm (No appreciable reduction)

Feed analysis and muck analysis: Presence of sulfur, bacteria and water found in oil sample and Fe, SRB found in muck

Third party damage: Frequent but failure not reported

Due to seismic zone, pipe cover is 1.5 meter and thickness more than 14.2 mm. No earthquake reported

River crossing, wash out occurred due to flood, bank protection provided

Safety interlocks failed occasionally but pipeline failure not reported. Attended promptly

Questions:

1. Identify threats and existing control measures.

2. Based on existing control measures and inference, assess the risk, and carry out risk assessment and suggest risk management plan

Ans 1. Threats and control measures :

Sl No	Segment	Parameters	Inference	Action plan
1	External corrosion	CP Status	OK	Monitoring
		Coating surveys	Coating defect	To be repaired
		ILI	Not done	To be done
		NDT	Thickness ok at terminal	Monitoring
2	Internal corrosion	ILI	Not done	To be done
		Corrosion rate	5 mpy	Monitoring
		Product and muck analysis	S, water, SRB, Fe found	Injection of corrosion inhibitor and biocides
3	Third party damage	Frequency of incidents	Frequent, No failure	Regular patrolling, Awareness program
4	SCC	Detection of crack	Not done	Crack detection to be done
5	Manufacturing & construction defect	Welding defect, crack, dent	ILI and crack detection not done	To be done
6	Operation fault	Failure of safety devices	Occasional	Regular testing
7	Weather related	Incident of earthquake, flood, lightening	Washout occurred. No failure	Repair required. Physical inspection

Risk assessment and risk management plan

Sl No	Segment	Parameters	Inference	Prob	Imp	Risk Rating	Risk Management Plan
1	External corrosion	CP Status	OK	Low	Mod	Low	Monitoring
		Coating defect	Yes	Mod	Mod	Mod	Repair of coating defect
		Metal loss	Not done	Mod	Mod	Mod	ILI and NDT to be done
2	Internal corrosion	Metal loss	Not done	High	Mod	High	ILI and NDT to be done
		Product and muck analysis	S, water, SRB, Fe found	High	Mod	High	Injection of corrosion inhibitor and biocides
3	Third party damage	Frequency of incidents	Frequent, No failure	Mod	Mod	Mod	Regular patrolling
4	SCC	Detection of crack	Not done	Mod	Mod	Mod	Inspection by SCC tool
5	Manufacturing defect	Welding defect,	ILI and crack	Mod	Mod	Mod	ILI to be done

		crack, dent	detection not done				
6	Operation fault	Failure of safety devices	Occasional	Mod	Mod	Mod	Regular testing
7	Weather related	Earthquake flood, lightening	Washout				Regular patrolling and physical inspection

Case study 2:

Following is data of wet and sour, onshore gas pipeline.

Pipe diameter 152.4 mm

Wall thickness 12.6 mm

API 5LX 52

Length 5.75 Km

SMYS 358 MPa

Year of commissioning 1996

Design life 20 years,

MAOP 115Kg/Cm2

Design temperature 60 degrees C

Pipeline integrity assessment data is as follows:

ILI done in 2011

CP monitoring was done quarterly for ON potential

No OFF potential measurement was done

CIPL, CAT and DCVG survey were done in 2015 and reported both overprotection and under protection and minor coating defects. Corrective measures were taken to maintain protection level.

No coating was repaired.

No record for cleaning pigging and feed and pig residue analysis were available.

Coupon was installed at terminal from top and its corrosion rate was less than 1 mpy.

Wash out and exposure were reported due to excess rain and flood but timely rectification was done and failure was averted.

Patrolling of pipeline was done continuously by security guards with GPS tracking system.

Instrument calibration schedule was maintained quarterly.

Performance test of safety valves was done annually.

EGP was done before commissioning and no defect was observed.

Questions:

1. Based on the data and considering all threats, find out the gaps in integrity assessment plan and suggest improvement in the system.

Gaps in integrity assessment plan and recommendations

Sl No	Threats	Integrity assessment plan	Gaps in integrity assessment	Recommendations
1	External	ON OFF	OFF	OFF potential

	corrosion	potential measurement	potential measurement not done	measurement to be done once in a year
		Coating integrity surveys	None	No recommendation
		ILI	Due in 2016, not done	Immediate and every five years
2	Internal corrosion	ILI	Due in 2016, not done	Immediate and every five years
		Corrosion monitoring by coupon/ER probes	Coupons was not installed at 6 o clock position	Coupon is required to be installed at 6 o clock position
		Product and muck analysis	No record was available	Feed gas analysis should be done once in a year and muck analysis after each cleaning
		Cleaning pigging	No record was available	Cleaning pigging should be done once in a year
3	Third party damage	Patrolling by security guards with	None	No recommendatio

		GPS tracking system		n
4	SCC	SCC tools	Not done	Crack detection by SCC tool to be done
5	Manufacturing &construction defect	EGP before commissioning and NDT inspection	None	No recommendation
6	Operation fault	Calibration of instruments and performance test of safety valves	None	No recommendation
7	Weather and environment related	Inspection of vulnerable locations	None	No recommendation

Case study 3:

The parameters of a gas pipeline

Outside diameter	812.8 mm
Grade	API 5L X 65
Wall thickness	19.10 mm
MAOP	135 bar
Design temperature	75 degree C

SMTS	530.9 N/mm2
Year of Commissioning	2000
Length	60 km
Pipeline product	Natural Gas
Pipe thickness in 2005	16.28 mm
Pipe thickness in 2015	14.32 mm
Length of defect	200 mm
Safety class	Medium

Questions

1. Calculate critical pressure in 2015 and draw an inference whether pipeline strength was safe in 2015?

2. Also calculate remaining life and draw an inference whether pipeline is safe in 2019

3. Also calculate ERF

Answers:

1. Corrosion growth rate as per API 570=(19.10-14.32)/ 15 = 4.78/15 = 0.31 mm/year or 12.2 mpy. The corrosion rate is high

Critical pressure $P_r = \dfrac{[\Upsilon m*2t*fu\,(1-\Upsilon d(d/t)*]}{(D-t)\left(1-\dfrac{\Upsilon d\,(d/t)*}{Q}\right)}$

(d/t) * = (d/t) measured + εd* StD (d/t)

d = 4.78 mm, t = 19.10 mm and StD (d/t) = 0.08, εd = 1
(d/t) *= 0.25 + 1*.08 = 0.33
Q =√1+0.31(l/√D*t) ^{2}, D = 812. 8 mm and l = 200 mm
Q = √ {1+0.31 (200/√812.8*19.10) ^{2} = 1.34
ϒm = 0.85, ϒd = 1.28

fu= (SMTS-fu temp) *άu = (530.9-15) *0.96 = 495.3 N/mm2

$$P_r = \frac{0.85*2*19.10*495.3(1-1.28*0.33}{(812.8-19.10) * (1- \frac{1.28*0.33)}{1.34}}$$

= 17.08 Newton/mm² or 174.2 Kg/Cm² which is more than 1.10*135 Kg/Cm2 that is 148.5 Kg/Cm2, hence pipe is safe at this pressure.

2. Critical depth is calculated at corrosion length of 200 mm at the critical pressure of 1.10*135 Kg/Cm2 that is 148.5 Kg/Cm2 or 14.5 N/mm2. Critical depth d comes to 7.43 mm or 38.9 % of original thickness. As the length and metal loss both increase, the critical pressure will decrease. Here, referring to DNV RP F101 graph for residual life assessment, metal loss is predicted at 33% and length at 260 mm for the next period of 4.5 years from 2015 to reach critical pressure. Thus, life is up more than six months from 2019. It is safe in 2019

3. ERF = 148.5/174.2 = 0.85

Case study 4:

Following is data of wet and sour, onshore gas pipeline.

Pipe diameter 152.4 mm

Wall thickness 12.6 mm

API 5LX 52

Length 5.75 Km

SMYS 358 MPa

Year of commissioning 1996

Design life 20 years

MAOP 115Kg/Cm2

Design temperature 60 degrees C

Pipeline integrity assessment data is as follows:

ILI done in 2011: External metal loss at Ch 22.30 was inside terminal @ 40 % and length of metal loss at 90 mm. internal corrosion was found at Ch 5819.14 @ 25 % of 12.6 mm with length metal loss at 60 mm

Questions:

Find out fitness of pipe in 2019 and residual life based on 2011 data.

Suggest rectification measures based on fitness and residual life

Answer:

Corrosion rate = .40* 12.6/15 = 0.33 mm/year.

Fitness in 2019 can be found by taking metal loss @ 0.33 mm/year in 2019 at 7.68 (60%) and length of metal loss @ 6 mm/year at 138 mm and calculating critical pressure by the formula as below:

$$P_r = \frac{[\Upsilon m*2t*fu\ (1-\Upsilon d(d/t)*]}{(D-t)\ (1-\frac{\Upsilon d(d/t)*)}{Q}}$$

Critical pressure comes to 10.30 N/mm2 which is less than 1.1* 115 Kg/Cm2 or 12.40 N/mm2. Hence, pipe is not fit for use in 2019

Regarding residual life, after 3 years, depth and length come to 6.03 mm (47.6%) and 108 mm. At this juncture, critical pressure is 29.33 N/mm2 which is more than 12.40 N/mm2, hence pipe is acceptable. Residual life is 3 years more from 2011 that is up to 2014.

Based on the residual life up to 2014, it was required to replace or repair the metal loss part by composite wrap or full encirclement welded split sleeve.

Chapter 14

Quiz test on integrity management of onshore and offshore pipelines

Time allowed 45 minutes

1. Name five objectives of integrity management
2. Name five threats
3. Match contents of table 1 to table 2

Sl No	Table 1 for risks	Sl No	Table 2 for risk mitigation
1	Shop floor testing inaccuracies	1	Review by Consultant
2	Design inaccuracies	2	Line patrolling
3	Welding defects	3	ILI
4	Third party damage	4	TPIA quality check
5	Internal corrosion	5	100 % radiography

4. Impact due to pipeline failures

i increases as MAOP increases

ii decreases as outside diameter of pipeline increases

iii increases as population density increases

iv decreases as fire and explosion hazards decreases

A. i and ii only

B. i, iii and iv only

C. ii, iii and iv only

D. All of the above

5. Risk is defined as product of likelihood of failure and consequence of failure.

i True

ii False

6. Risk assessment is done to prioritize the pipeline section for integrity assessment and mitigation.

i True

ii False

7. As per SP 0106-2006, App A, the maximum quantity of H2S present in gas should be 5.7 mg/m^3.

i True

ii False

8. ERF should be more than 1 for safety of pipeline

i True

ii False

9. Which of the following corrective action is recommended for severe external metal loss?

i Pressure reduction

ii Pipe replacement

iii Type 'B' pressurized sleeve

iv Type 'A' reinforcing sleeve

A. i and ii only

B. i, ii and iii only

C. ii, iii and iv only

D. All of the above

10. Name five O&M data requirements for risk assessment

11. Safety class for Natural Gas terminal is medium

i True

ii False

12. What is preferable to control for lowering the risk of failure

i Probability of failure

ii Impact of failure

13. Match contents of table 1 to table 2. There can be multiple choices.

Sl No	Table 1 for threats	Sl No	Table 2 for integrity assessment tools

1	External corrosion	1	Schedule calibration and testing
2	Internal corrosion	2	Frequency of washout and exposure
3	Third party damage	3	Coating integrity surveys
4	Weather related	4	ILI
5	O&M related	5	NDT

14. During close interval potential survey, a drop was noticed in both ON and OFF potential and both was below protection level. Do you anticipate coating defect?

i Yes

ii No

15. In above example, which of the following would you suggest?

i Coating repair if coating defect is suspected

ii Off potential above protection level -0.85 V

iii Both of the above

iv None of the above

16. As per SP 0106-2006, App A, the maximum quantity of Co2 present in gas should be 3 volume %

iii True

iv False

17. Critical pressure should be more than 1.1 times MAOP for safety of pipeline

i True

ii False

18. Match contents of table 1 to table 2. There can be multiple choices

Sl No	Table 1 Integrity assessment tools	Sl No	Table 2 what to look out for
1	NDT	1	Welding defects, dents, gauges
2	CIPL, CAT & DCVG	2	Pipe strength
3	ILI	3	Metal loss
4	Pressure testing	4	Coating adequacy
5	Feed analysis	5	Presence of corrosive constituents

19. Which of the following statement is correct?

i Indirect inspection tool can be applied for cased crossing and disbanded coating

ii Two indirect tools shall be applied for detecting coating holidays

iii Only CAT survey can be applied for under paved road and rocky terrain

iv CIPL survey cannot be used for large holidays

A. i and ii only

B. ii and iii only

C. ii, iii and iv only

D. All of the above

20. Which of the following causes of internal corrosion are correct?

i Internal coating of piggable pipeline

ii Higher elevation

iii Higher temperature

iv Higher inclination angle

A. i and ii only

B. ii, iii and iv only

C. i, iii and iv only

D. All of the above

21. Steel pipe thickness was 9.4 mm in 2006 when pipeline was commissioned. ILI was done in 2014. The internal maximum wall thickness loss was 60 % of original wall thickness. Critical pressure was calculated as 100 Kg/Cm2 while MAOP was 90 Kg/Cm2. What was corrosion rate and ERF in 2014? What corrective action would you suggest based on ERF value?

22. Match contents of table 1 to table 2. There can be multiple choices.

Sl No	Table 1 Integrity assessment tools	Sl No	Table 2 Frequency
1	Feed quality analysis	1	Once in 5 years
2	Cleaning pigging for crude oil line	2	Once in 10 years
3	ILI for wet natural gas	3	Once in 6 months
4	Muck analysis for crude oil	4	Once in a year
5	Pressure testing	5	Once in 3 months

23. Internal corrosion is pre-dominant between 4 o clock and 8 o clock position

i True

ii False

24. Match contents of table 1 to table 2 and Table 3.

Sl No	Table 1 Interpretation	Sl No	Table 2 Integrity Assessment	Sl No	Table 3 Response
1	ERF≥0.8<1.0	1	Low	1	Immediate

2	ERF<0.8	2	Severe	2	Monitoring
3	ERF>1.0	3	Moderate	3	Schedule

25. Corrosion rate increases as inclination angle decreases
i True
ii False

26. Which of the following corrective action is recommended for severe internal corrosion?
i Pressure reduction
ii Pipe replacement
iii 'Type B' pressurized sleeve
iv 'Type A' reinforcing sleeve
A. i and iii only
B. i, ii and iii only
C. ii, iii and iv only
D. All of the above

27. Corrosion rate is measured more than 5.5 mpy. Corrosion rate is
i Low
ii Medium
iii High
iv Severe

28. Which one of the following is corrosion monitoring tool?
i ILI
ii Scrapper pigging
iii Corrosion coupon or ER probe
iv NDT
A. i, ii and iii only
B. ii, iii and iv only
C. i, iii and iv only
D. All of the above

Answers:

3. 1 to 4, 2 to1, 3 to 5, 4 to 2, 5 to 3
4. B
5. i
6. i
7. i
8. ii
9. D
11. ii
12. i
13. 1 to 3,4,5, 2 to 4,5, 3 to 4,5, 4 to 2, 5 to1
14. i
15. iii
16. ii
17. i
18. 1 to 2,3, 2 to 4, 3 to 1,2,3, 4 to 2, 5 to 5
19. B
20. C
21. 0.7 mm/year, 0.9, Schedule Pressure reduction/Repair/Replacement
22. 1 to 4, 2 to 5, 3 to 1, 4 to 5, 5 to 1
23. i
24. 1 to 3 to 3, 2 to 1 to 2, 3 to 2 to 1
25. ii
26. B
27. iii
28. C

Reference:

As per Art 1.4 referred standards

Printed by Libri Plureos GmbH in Hamburg,
Germany